COMPOSER SHOWCASE

HAL LEONARD STUDENT PIANO LIBRARY

An Awesome Adventure

EIGHT ORIGINAL PIANO SOLOS

BY LYNDA LYBECK-ROBINSON

CONTENTS

ISBN 978-1-4950-0023-2

HAL•LEONARD® CORPORATION

7777 W. BLUEMOUND RD. P.O. BOX 13819 MILWAUKEE, WI 53213

In Australia Contact:
Hal Leonard Australia Pty. Ltd.
4 Lentara Court
Cheltenham, Victoria, 3192 Australia
Email: ausadmin@halleonard.com.au

Visit Hal Leonard Online at
www.halleonard.com

Awesomeness

By Lynda Lybeck-Robinson

D.C. al Coda

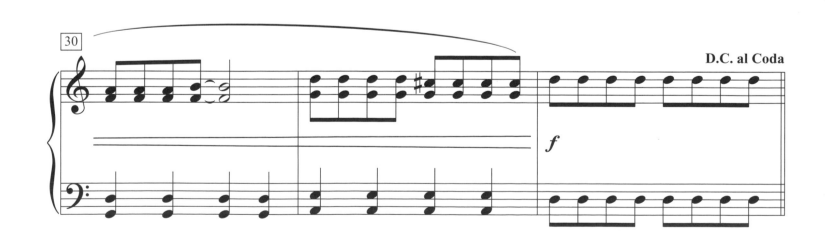

Combat in Space

By Lynda Lybeck-Robinson

Swift and brave (♩ = 100)
Last time play both hands 8va

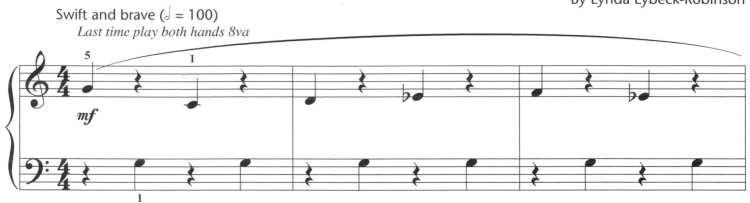

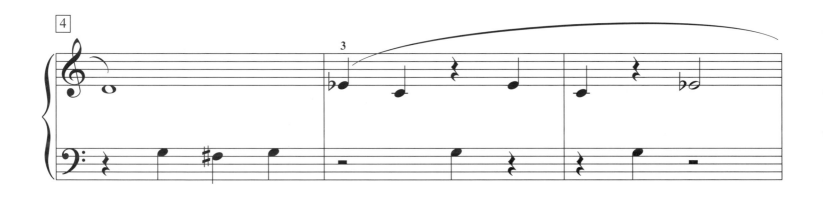

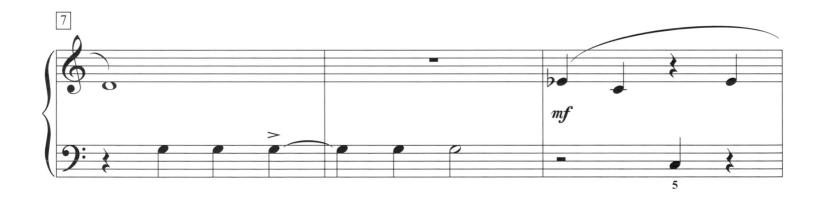

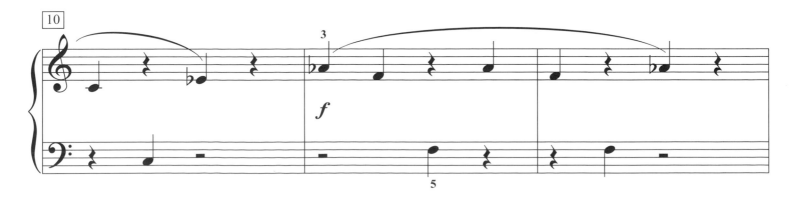

(Zero in on target!)

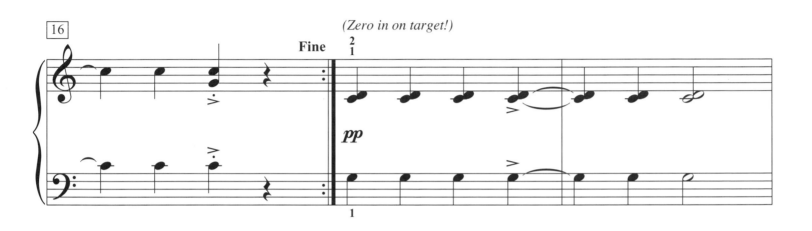

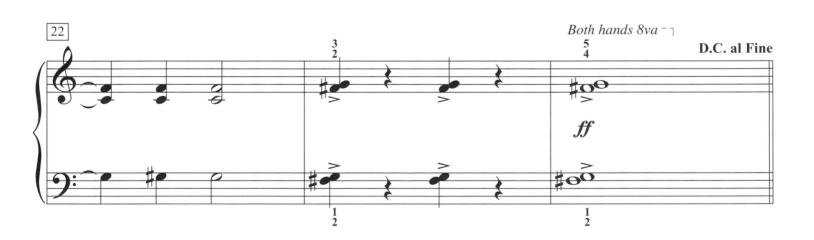

Dream Flyer

By Lynda Lybeck-Robinson

Eye of Horus

By Lynda Lybeck-Robinson

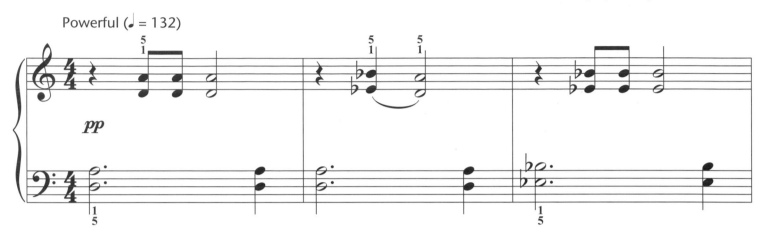

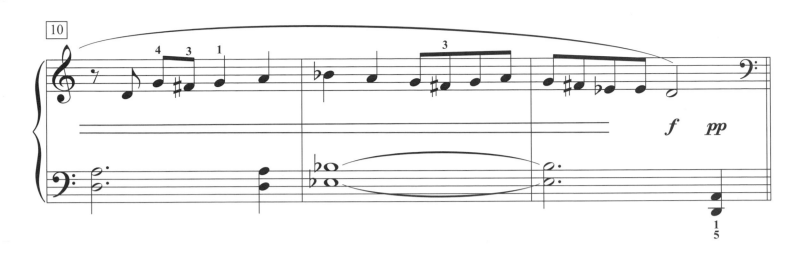

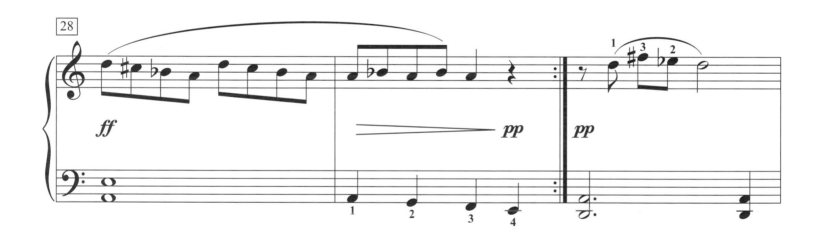

Hooligans

By Lynda Lybeck-Robinson

Sneaky Startling Fun (♩ = 100)
Both hands 8vb

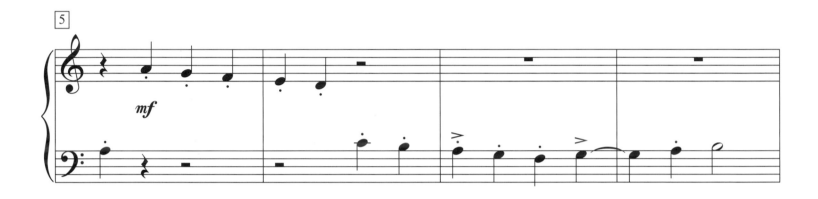

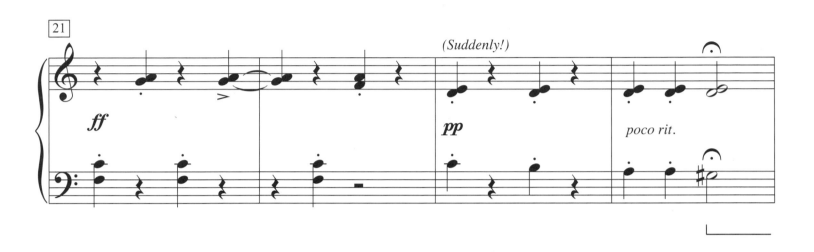

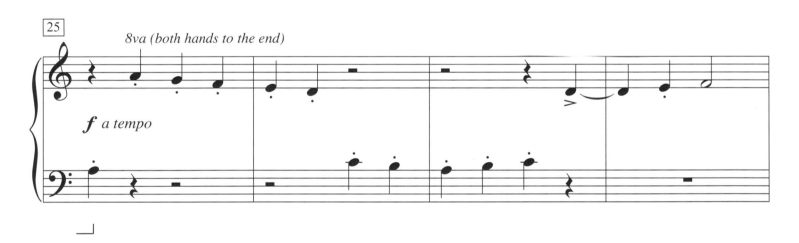

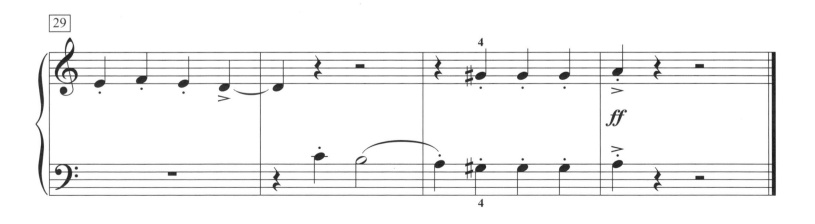

Pet Dragon

By Lynda Lybeck-Robinson

League of Champions

By Lynda Lybeck-Robinson

Proud and strong (♩ = 132)

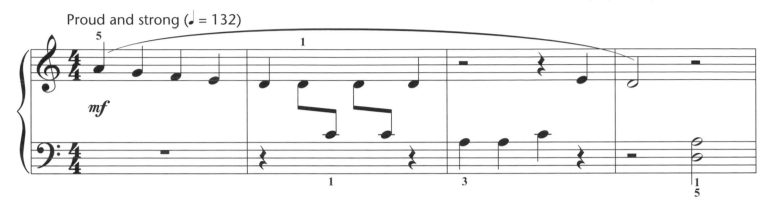

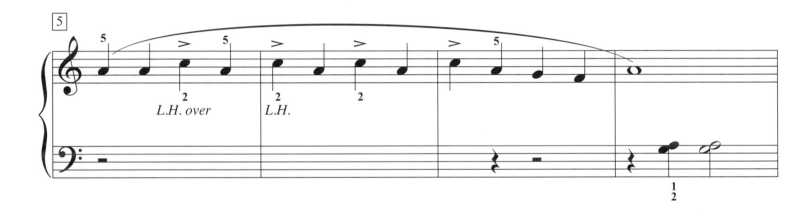

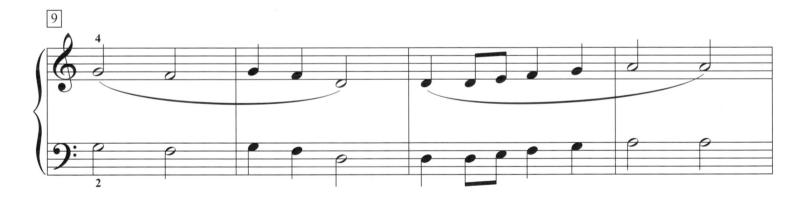

8vb _ ⌐

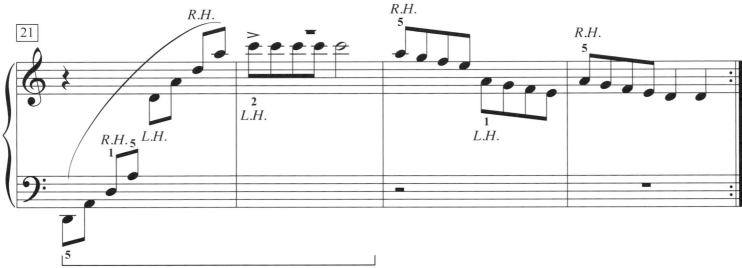

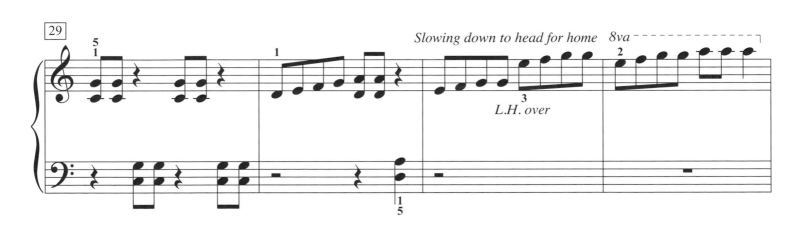

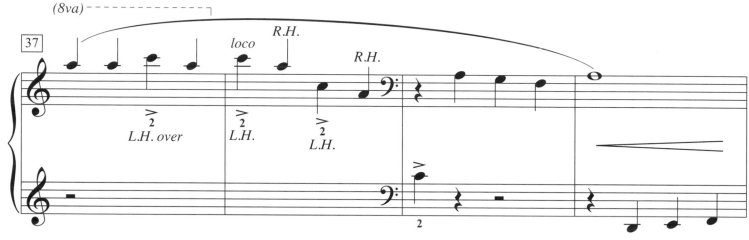

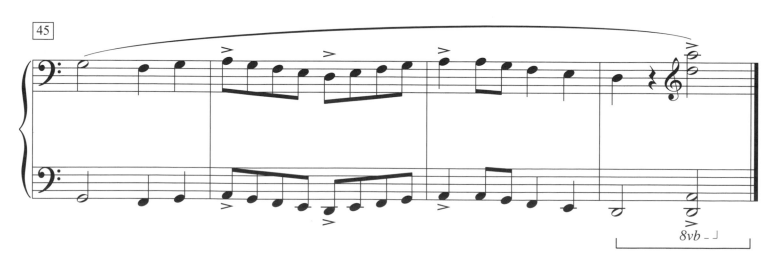

Surfin' Attitude

with optional buddy duet

By Lynda Lybeck-Robinson

Rockin' a beach attitude (♩ = 88)

(Snap!)   (Snap!)   (Snap!)   (Snap!)

Cool breeze un - der the palm trees.

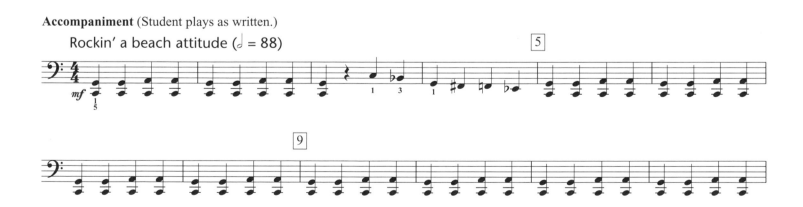

Hot sand be - tween my toes.

Accompaniment (Student plays as written.)

Rockin' a beach attitude (♩ = 88)

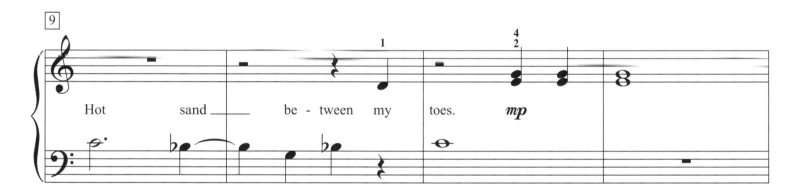

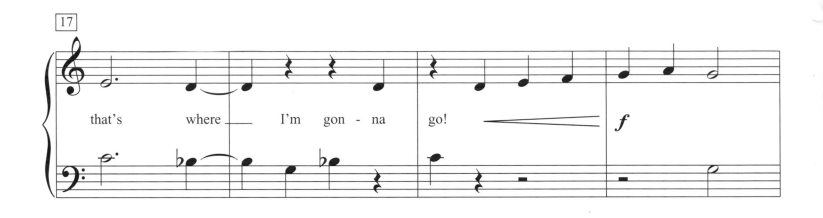

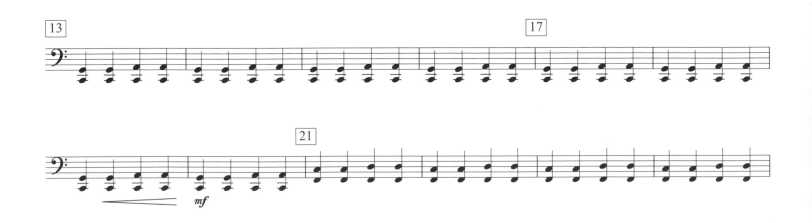

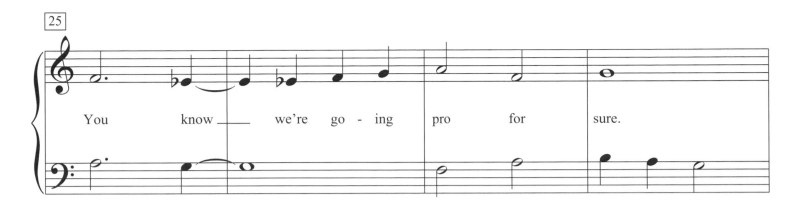

You know _____ we're go - ing pro for sure.

Watch me, _____ the wave is call - ing. _____

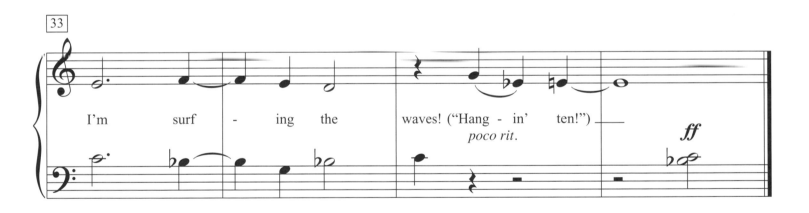

I'm surf - ing the waves! ("Hang - in' ten!") _____
poco rit.

ff

poco rit.

f

COMPOSER SHOWCASE
HAL LEONARD STUDENT PIANO LIBRARY

This series showcases great original piano music from our **Hal Leonard Student Piano Library** family of composers, including Bill Boyd, Phillip Keveren, Carol Klose, Jennifer Linn, Mona Rejino, Eugénie Rocherolle and more. Carefully graded for easy selection, each book contains gems that are certain to become classics!

BILL BOYD

JAZZ BITS (AND PIECES)
Early Intermediate Level
00290312 11 Solos......................$7.99

JAZZ DELIGHTS
Intermediate Level
00240435 11 Solos......................$7.99

JAZZ FEST
Intermediate Level
00240436 10 Solos......................$7.99

JAZZ PRELIMS
Early Elementary Level
00290032 12 Solos......................$6.99

JAZZ SKETCHES
Intermediate Level
00220001 8 Solos........................$7.99

JAZZ STARTERS
Elementary Level
00290425 10 Solos......................$6.99

JAZZ STARTERS II
Late Elementary Level
00290434 11 Solos......................$7.99

JAZZ STARTERS III
Late Elementary Level
00290465 12 Solos......................$7.99

THINK JAZZ!
Early Intermediate Level
00290417 Method Book...............$10.99

DEBORAH BRADY

PUPPY DOG TALES
Elementary Level
00296718 5 Solos........................$6.95

TONY CARAMIA

JAZZ MOODS
Intermediate Level
00296728 8 Solos........................$6.95

SUITE DREAMS
Intermediate Level
00296775 4 Solos........................$6.99

SONDRA CLARK

DAKOTA DAYS
Intermediate Level
00296521 5 Solos........................$6.95

FAVORITE CAROLS FOR TWO
Intermediate Level
00296530 5 Duets.......................$7.99

FLORIDA FANTASY SUITE
Intermediate Level
00296766 3 Duets.......................$7.95

ISLAND DELIGHTS
Intermediate Level
00296666 4 Solos........................$6.95

THREE ODD METERS
Intermediate Level
00296472 3 Duets.......................$6.95

For full descriptions and song lists for the books listed here, and to view a complete list of titles in this series, please visit our website at www.halleonard.com

MATTHEW EDWARDS

CONCERTO FOR YOUNG PIANISTS
FOR 2 PIANOS, FOUR HANDS
Intermediate Level Book/CD
00296356 3 Movements $16.95

CONCERTO NO. 2 IN G MAJOR
FOR 2 PIANOS, 4 HANDS
Intermediate Level Book/CD
00296670 3 Movements................$16.95

PHILLIP KEVEREN

MOUSE ON A MIRROR
Late Elementary Level
00296361 5 Solos........................$6.95

MUSICAL MOODS
Elementary/Late Elementary Level
00296714 7 Solos........................$5.95

ROMP!
A DIGITAL KEYBOARD ENSEMBLE FOR SIX PLAYERS
Intermediate Level
00296549 Book/CD......................$9.95

SHIFTY-EYED BLUES
Late Elementary Level
00296374 5 Solos........................$6.99

TEX-MEX REX
Late Elementary Level
00296353 6 Solos........................$6.99

CAROL KLOSE

CORAL REEF SUITE
Late Elementary Level
00296354 7 Solos........................$6.99

DESERT SUITE
Intermediate Level
00296667 6 Solos........................$7.99

FANCIFUL WALTZES
Early Intermediate Level
00296473 5 Solos........................$7.95

GARDEN TREASURES
Late Intermediate Level
00296787 5 Solos........................$7.99

ROMANTIC EXPRESSIONS
Intermediate/Late Intermediate Level
00296923 5 Solos........................$8.99

WATERCOLOR MINIATURES
Early Intermediate Level
00296848 7 Solos........................$7.99

JENNIFER LINN

AMERICAN IMPRESSIONS
Intermediate Level
00296471 6 Solos........................$7.99

CHRISTMAS IMPRESSIONS
Intermediate Level
00296706 8 Solos........................$6.99

JUST PINK
Elementary Level
00296722 9 Solos........................$6.99

LES PETITES IMAGES
Late Elementary Level
00296664 7 Solos........................$7.99

LES PETITES IMPRESSIONS
Intermediate Level
00296355 6 Solos........................$7.99

REFLECTIONS
Late Intermediate Level
00296843 5 Solos........................$7.99

TALES OF MYSTERY
Intermediate Level
00296769 6 Solos........................$7.99

MONA REJINO

CIRCUS SUITE
Late Elementary Level
00296665 5 Solos........................$5.95

JUST FOR KIDS
Elementary Level
00296840 8 Solos........................$7.99

MERRY CHRISTMAS MEDLEYS
Intermediate Level
00296799 5 Solos........................$7.99

PORTRAITS IN STYLE
Early Intermediate Level
00296507 6 Solos........................$7.99

EUGÉNIE ROCHEROLLE

ENCANTOS ESPAÑOLES (SPANISH DELIGHTS)
Intermediate Level
00125451 6 Solos........................$7.99

JAMBALAYA
FOR 2 PIANOS, 8 HANDS
Intermediate Level
00296654 Piano Ensemble.............$9.99

JAMBALAYA
FOR 2 PIANOS, 4 HANDS
Intermediate Level
00296725 Piano Duo (2 Pianos) $7.95

TOUR FOR TWO
Late Elementary Level
00296832 6 Duets.......................$7.99

TREASURES
Late Elementary/Early Intermediate Level
00296924 7 Solos........................$8.99

CHRISTOS TSITSAROS

DANCES FROM AROUND THE WORLD
Early Intermediate Level
00296688 7 Solos........................$6.95

LYRIC BALLADS
Intermediate/Late Intermediate Level
00102404 6 Solos........................$8.99

POETIC MOMENTS
Intermediate Level
00296403 8 Solos........................$8.99

SONATINA HUMORESQUE
Late Intermediate Level
00296772 3 Movements $6.99

SONGS WITHOUT WORDS
Intermediate Level
00296506 9 Solos........................$7.95

THROUGHOUT THE YEAR
Late Elementary Level
00296723 12 Duets.....................$6.95

ADDITIONAL COLLECTIONS

ALASKA SKETCHES
by Lynda Lybeck-Robinson
Early Intermediate Level
00119637 8 Solos........................$7.99

AMERICAN PORTRAITS
by Wendy Stevens
Intermediate Level
00296817 6 Solos........................$7.99

AT THE LAKE
by Elvina Pearce
Elementary/Late Elementary Level
00131642 10 Solos and Duets.......$7.99

COUNTY RAGTIME FESTIVAL
by Fred Kern
Intermediate Level
00296882 7 Rags........................$7.99

PLAY THE BLUES!
by Luann Carman (Method Book)
Early Intermediate Level
00296357 10 Solos......................$9.99

HAL•LEONARD®
CORPORATION

7777 W. BLUEMOUND RD· P.O. BOX 13819 MILWAUKEE· WI 53213

0814